About the Bank Street Ready-to-Read Series

More than seventy-five years of educational research, innovative teaching, and quality publishing have earned The Bank Street College of Education its reputation as America's most trusted name in early childhood education.

Because no two children are exactly alike in their development, the Bank Street Ready-to-Read series is written on three levels to accommodate the individual stages of reading readiness of children ages three through eight.

○ *Level 1:* **Getting Ready to Read (Pre-K–Grade 1)**
Level 1 books are perfect for reading aloud with children who are getting ready to read or just starting to read words or phrases. These books feature large type, repetition, and simple sentences.

● *Level 2:* **Reading Together (Grades 1–3)**
These books have slightly smaller type and longer sentences. They are ideal for children beginning to read by themselves who may need help.

○ *Level 3:* **I Can Read It Myself (Grades 2–3)**
These stories are just right for children who can read independently. They offer more complex and challenging stories and sentences.

All three levels of The Bank Street Ready-to-Read books make it easy to select the books most appropriate for your child's development and enable him or her to grow with the series step by step. The levels purposely overlap to reinforce skills and further encourage reading.

We feel that making reading fun is the single most important thing anyone can do to help children become good readers. We hope you will become part of Bank Street's long tradition of learning through sharing.

The Bank Street College
of Education

To Jonathan Matthew Davies — W. H. H.

For Kitty — D. C.

For a free color catalog describing Gareth Stevens' list of high-quality books and multimedia programs, call 1-800-542-2595 (USA) or 1-800-461-9120 (Canada). Gareth Stevens Publishing's Fax: (414) 225-0377.
See our catalog, too, on the World Wide Web: http://gsinc.com

Library of Congress Cataloging-in-Publication Data

Hooks, William H.
    Feed me! : an Aesop fable / retold by William H. Hooks ; illustrated by Doug Cushman.
      p. cm. -- (Bank Street ready-to-read)
    Adaptation of: The lark in the cornfield.
    Summary: A mother lark whose nest in the farmer's corn is threatened by the coming harvest uses wisdom in deciding when to move her babies.
    ISBN 0-8368-1616-1 (lib. bdg.)
    [1. Fables.] I. Aesop. II. Cushman, Doug, ill. III. Title. IV. Series.
PZ8.2.H64Fe 1996
398.24'528812--dc20
[E]   96-6879

This edition first published in 1996 by
Gareth Stevens Publishing
1555 North RiverCenter Drive, Suite 201
Milwaukee, Wisconsin 53212 USA

© 1992 by Byron Preiss Visual Publications, Inc. Text © 1992 by Bank Street College of Education. Illustrations © 1992 by Doug Cushman and Byron Preiss Visual Publications, Inc.

Published by arrangement with Bantam Doubleday Dell Books for Young Readers, a division of Bantam Doubleday Dell Publishing Group, Inc., New York, New York. All rights reserved.

BANK STREET READY TO READ™ is a trademark of Bantam Doubleday Dell Books For Young Readers, a division of Bantam Doubleday Dell Publishing Group, Inc.

Printed in Mexico

1 2 3 4 5 6 7 8 9 99 98 97 96

Bank Street Ready-to-Read™

Feed Me!
An Aesop Fable

Retold by William H. Hooks
Illustrated by Doug Cushman

A Byron Preiss Book

Gareth Stevens Publishing
MILWAUKEE

A mother lark made a nest
in a cornfield.
She laid four beautiful eggs.

"Soon I'll have
four beautiful babies,"
she said.
And soon she did.

As the corn grew,
so did the babies.
They were always hungry.
The mother lark spent all day
looking for food.

Whenever the babies saw her
they chirped . . .

The corn grew tall
and the baby birds grew big.
They chirped
louder than ever...

The mother lark began
to worry.
Soon the corn would be ripe.
The farmer would come
to cut it.
What would become
of her babies?

"Watch for the farmer,"
the mother bird said
to her babies.
The babies said...

"Listen to the farmer,"
she warned.
The babies said...

10

"Tell me everything you hear,"
said the mother bird.
The babies chirped...

WE WILL
TELL!

So the mother lark flew away
to look for food.

When she came home
the babies were very hungry.
They chirped...

The mother bird said,
"First, tell me:
Did you watch for the farmer?"
The babies chirped...

Then they all said together...

"Wait!" said the mother lark.
"Did you listen?
What did the farmer say?"
The baby birds cried...

15

"There is no need to be scared,"
said the mother lark.
"Neighbors are not so quick
to cut corn for someone else."
Then she fed her hungry babies.

The next day the mother lark
flew off again for food.
"Watch, listen, and
tell me everything,"
she said.

When she returned to the nest,
the babies were hiding.
"It is only me," said the lark.
"What did you see today?"

The babies cried...

Then they all
chirped together...

"Wait," said the mother lark.
"Tell me what you heard."
The babies chirped...

"Don't worry," said the mother.
"Friends will be slow to come
and cut the corn."
Then she fed
her hungry babies.

The next day the mother lark
came home early
with fat worms
for the baby birds.
The babies cried…

"Not yet," said the mother lark.
"What did you see today?"

"What did you hear?"
asked the mother lark.
The babies cried...

The mother lark
looked worried.
The babies cried…

"Eat quickly!"
said the mother lark.
"Tonight we will move.
When people do
their own work,
things get done."

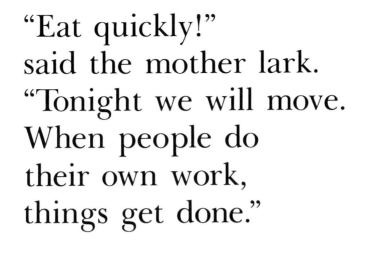

So the mother lark
moved her babies
to the woods
that very night.